From Paycheck-to-Paycheck to Financial Freedom

Things You Never Learned From School About Financial Intelligence

Brigham Ramsey

Table Of Contents

Get Your Free Audiobook

As a way of saying thank you for purchasing this book, I am giving you a free audiobook copy of *"From Paycheck-to-Paycheck to Financial Freedom: Things You Never Learned From School About Financial Intelligence"* so that you can listen and learn from this book even if you are doing something else. Yes, you read it right, this is free, and this gift is exclusive only to the readers of this book. This audiobook is free only for readers who are not yet subscribed to Audible.

https://becomingwealthyandhappy.com/fpp2ff-gift-audiobook

Another Free Gift

Already have an Audible account? I have another gift for you, which is a downloadable pdf copy of "The Ultimate *Budget Planner*" that you can use and print at home. You can start your journey to being financially free by learning how to budget with the help of this planner.

https://becomingwealthyandhappy.com/fpp2ff-gift-pdf-planner

Introduction

Robby fidgeted nervously as he sat in line, waiting for his turn. He rubbed a spot on his black shoes and straightened out his coat. If he was going to succeed on this most important interview, he had to be no less than perfect. He shuffled his papers, turning them over and over again. He knew his credentials were good, but were they good enough? He graduated with honors with a degree in Accounting and Business Management, a course his father wanted him to have. Robby became the youngest editor-in-chief of the college paper, a distinction his mother goaded him to achieve. He worked his way to graduation with stellar marks, few friends, and a big dream. And today, all these sleepless nights, these high honors and hard work would all cumulate in this one interview. It was a long wait, and it made Robby more nervous. In these uneasy moments, questions start to pester his patience. "Is this career in accounting what I really want to do? If I get accepted here, will I really reach my dreams? Do I see myself in an office desk day in and day out for the rest of my working life?" The questions were disturbing Robby's composure.

Martha clocked in at exactly 6:59 AM. She always kept to the time, never going beyond the 7 AM cut. She kept to her schedule, fearing that something would go wrong if she went to the office later than usual. Martha went to her cubicle and started fixing her things for the day. She needed to retrieve the documents for this morning's meeting. There were a number of errands to do and Martha liked to arrange them into post-its by color of priority. At noon, her boss would have lunch outside so she had time to pay the bills. She could squeeze in paying for the electricity and water bills. The afternoon was reserved for answering all the emails. Martha's day was quite fixed and this had been the order for ten years already. As she clocked in, Martha knew that her day would go by in exactly the same way as every day. Perhaps, she loved the comfort of the routine, and the predictability of a paycheck. But there were moments in a day when she had a nagging feeling amidst the peace of predictability. Was it all worth it? Is this how I want to live the rest of my life? What happens when the paycheck ends? Rather than face the questions, Martha comforted herself with typing a few more memos and answered a call.

The box was almost full when Bruce made one last sweep of his cubicle. It was his last day at the office and he felt a little bit nostalgic. He couldn't imagine spending forty years of his life chained to that small desk, typing away all those records, answering irate clients and tiptoeing around bosses. He could remember the first day he showed up for an interview. After forty years, he still dreaded interviews with whichever boss he had to report to. Now, all that was all gone. Plus, the assurance of a paycheck. Bruce felt a little relief in leaving a place that has tired him all these years. But he also feared facing the unknown of retirement. He had saved some money. But he didn't know if that was enough to last him the next ten years. He could probably start a business. He could invest in stocks. There were a lot of possibilities, but Bruce was utterly lost. While he dreaded every day of his life in the office, he couldn't imagine a day without it. Where would he go now? What happens next? With much trepidation, Bruce carried his box out of the office towards the unknown.

These situations may be your own story right now. At any stage of our lives, we are always confronted with questions related especially to money. You may deny its influence on you, but you cannot totally be free from how financial matters can impact your life. You may be a young upstart, fresh from college, and wondering which job will fit you or which employer will even hire you? Or you could be in a job right now that pays the bills, but you still worry about the sustainability of your income. Or you might already be nearing retirement and you are wondering what to do next, how to enjoy your savings but also have enough to last you through your golden years. We all worry about finances, that is one fact we cannot escape. And yet, the questions we raise are not answered, or worse, not acknowledged.

Financial sustainability then for most of us is achieved in the usual employee pathway. We enter into the capitalist system as workers with wages. We try to fit ourselves in the system through a combination of talent, preference, opportunity, network and sheer luck. We slave away in the capitalist system, at times being promoted in some hierarchical fashion, as we gain years, experience and influence. Our jobs pay the bills, take care of the housing, give us the assurance of food, help us dream of sending our kids to good schools and enjoy some leisure. We need the employee pathway because it is the only system that we are exposed to, that we know works that we know we cannot escape from. We want the assurance of monthly paychecks because this is the only way we know how to live.

And it can remain this way for years without us questioning if it is actually sustainable. The beauty of this capitalist-employee system is that it works. Our bosses earn and we earn some. And that may be enough for us. But the illusion in this system only works if employees are satisfied with getting a paycheck. What capitalists and bosses are never telling you is that it is possible to earn as much as they are earning. They will give you some permanency of a salary, a variety of benefits for your family, a few perks and the assurance of a retirement pay. But they will never tell you that you can earn more than what you are actually earning. Bosses will not tell you that what you are getting is actually less than what you should be earning. Because if they do, the whole system collapses and everybody will end up earning the same.

No, this is not a book on social theory or some anti-capitalist propaganda. My goal for you is not to destroy a system or quit your current job now. My goal for all of you reading this book is that you may be financially free. By this, I do not just mean earning more. Financial wealth is part of being financially free but is not equal to it. Your freedom is not just in terms of having more money now. The freedom I want you to have consists of two concepts you need to learn, whether you are just starting to work, or even at your retiring age. Focusing only on having more money will lead you to short returns and unsustainable happiness. What I want you to learn is that to be financially free, you have to be FREE FROM and FREE FOR. These two are related concepts that we will define later on. They are very similar but not the same concepts. Both of them refer to financial freedom but tackle a different aspect of it.

Being financially free from is the standard approach to wealth we encounter when we go to business workshops or talk to lectures. When we say that a person is financially free, we are referring to the freedom we experience from certain limitations. We are successful when we are financially free from debts. You may have been a student who got student loans you then had to pay for the next twenty years. You may possess a number of cards where you got your housing and car loans. Or you may be indebted to a bank after loaning capital to start your own business. Whatever it is, you are successful only when you are free from these debts that hold you back. Most of us never go beyond this stage because we may be stuck in paying debts. We have accumulated debts that are beyond our capacity to pay, so the bills keep on mounting and mounting until we are buried six feet on the ground and our children inherit this load from us. We may have made foolish financial decisions in the past like collecting credit cards and not monitoring our cash outflow. Years after, we are suffering from the burden of debt until the last paycheck and probably beyond. This book will help you tackle how to get out of that debt trap so you can be totally free from.

Being free from is not only about debts, but everything that holds us back from living the life we want. This may be in the form of impulsive buying, poor investments, lack of financial foresight, or even overspending. Even the whole capitalist-employee system may be a hindrance to our freedom. Living paycheck to paycheck means having to slave away at a desk, totally dependent on a fixed salary. When that money pot runs out, you are financially crippled. Having a paycheck mentality also limits the amount of worth you are getting. By relying on a monthly salary, you are saying that you are only worth so and so a month. But actually, with your limitless potential, your salary far underestimates your true value. You should be in control of your earnings and not the other way around. There is a need to be free from these shackles that bind your true potential.

But the more neglected understanding of freedom is that it is not just a freedom from, but also a freedom for. Our work is not directed towards the past, of repaying what has been spent. We want to work towards some other purpose or objective and not just through the accumulation of wealth. We work very hard so that we can be free for many things: our dream house, the education of our children, the car we have always imagined buying, properties to manage and a comfortable life. We want to be free for accomplishing the things we love and are passionate about. Freedom for talks about goals, visions, and personal dreams. How do you want to live your life? What kind of life do you imagine for yourself and for the next generations?

We need to dwell on these two kinds of freedom in order to be truly free. Freedom from helps us escape the clutches of debt and non-sustainability. Freedom for directs our efforts towards some purpose. Only by being aware and committed to these two freedoms can we say that we are truly financially free. We are not saying that only money will give us this freedom. We are saying that money is one of the most important ways we can achieve this kind of freedom. This book will help you focus on achieving that financial freedom, from and for, that will give you the kind of life you have been wanting to have.

This book will also feature the lives of some of the wealthiest and most influential people in the world today. They have been topping the list in all financial magazines in terms of material wealth. There is a value in learning from their experiences to guide us in our journey towards financial freedom. You might be thinking that you are very different from them, that there is a billion to one chance that you would succeed the way that they did. But by reading their lives, you will see that many of them were not born in rich families or had big capital when they first started. A lot of them clawed their way through the very system we are all in and emerged on top. They may even be the bosses of your own bosses. Learning their lives will help us enter into their minds and allow us to imitate that for ourselves. Their mindsets, visions, practices, and way of thinking and living might rub off us when we begin to analyze how they are able to reach the success they dreamt of. Entering the minds of the rich will enrich us, making us realize that everything we set our mind to is possible.

My goal for you is to be truly financially free. I have seen a lot of people traverse that capitalist-employee pathway and have ended up with so-so lives. I, too, have gone through that pathway and I have felt that inner struggle staying in that trap. The realization that I didn't want to stay in this trap forever allowed me some sense of freedom. My hope is that I can share that freedom with you. We may be walking in different stages but there is no better time to take the road to financial freedom than today. This book will guide you through that difficult journey, the road-less traveled to financial freedom. Each chapter will tackle a different quality of financial freedom that you have to inculcate.

It will require a lot of openness from you as it will challenge some of the things you believe were true in terms of financial stability. It may shake some foundation, prodding you to question yourself. It may reveal vulnerabilities you may not know of. But the journey is in itself healing and enriching. Be open to this journey and see how it can transform your life into that which is more freeing.

Chapter 1: Mastering Your Impulses

The richest man in Mexico, Carlos Slim Helu, has not changed his house for the last 40 years. Carlos Slim owns a number of multinational companies, including America Movil, the biggest mobile phone operator in Latin America, Carso Oil and Gas, Sears Mexico and Immobilaria Carso. He has stakes in different companies such as the New York Times, Realia, Bankia, WellAware, and Telekom Austria among others. He is currently the 8th richest man in the Forbes 2019 list with a net worth of \$59.5 billion. But with such a great fortune, Carlos Slim Helu has not moved residences for the past 40 years.

Is this merely out of convenience? Most probably not since his industries are in major cities all over the world. His choice of residence is but a mere reflection of the kind of frugality Carlos Slim Helu has. He was born from immigrant parents from Lebanon and started working at an early age. Even at such a young age, Carlos Slim Helu knew that he had to make wise use of his money. He carried this frugality and business acumen in his studies and later on, going full time with acquiring a lot of companies.

His business style was simple: invest in low-value but high potential companies, improve it, and sell it for profit. During his time, many businesses were buying out and Carlos Slim Helu saw an opportunity. He began buying investments at a lower price and reselling them at higher ones. From this strategy, he was able to acquire industries ranging from stock brokerage to construction, to telecommunications. And at 79 years, he is still pushing the limits of investment with his good knack for business. His lifestyle remains simple and he prefers the usual comforts of his youth and family to energize him in his home.

What can we learn from this great man? Carlos Slim Helu's lifestyle and business decisions reflect a certain austerity, bordering on frugality even. He had put great value on money, and so he invested it only on things he knew held great value as well. The young 12 year old Carlos Slim Helu could have used up that money to buy himself a nice shirt or a tasty meal. A $20 could already buy for him a cool earphone set or a shiny fashionable belt buckle. He could have easily spent it on a round at the arcades or two heft pizza pies. Against the natural inclinations held by his peers, Carlos Slim Helu chose to invest his money on business. It may take some time to get a profit given his small investment, but it was the start of a billionaire journey anchored on frugality and wise financial thinking. Even at his old age, Carlos Slim Helu still proves that you don't need the biggest house or the trendiest accommodations to feel important. One just had to focus on the things one wanted to do.

This would be the only chapter that would discuss the concept of freedom from. The emphasis of the book is really to allow people to discover freedom for, the wise use of resources to achieve goals. But we cannot do this without the crucial step of learning how to be free from. Being financially free means mastering our own inclinations before we commit unwise financial decisions. This natural inclination refers to our innate drive for happiness. We want to be happy. We want to be satisfied. And our happiness will be varied and unique in each situation and across peoples. This is but natural. There are many ways to achieve this happiness. But there are ways that are more practical than others; there are others that lead us to unwise financial decisions.

For example, you work so hard for a whole month. You take a number of over times to finish a deadline. You take on too many projects and work sleepless nights. You feel so stressed for the entire month, bottling all that tension inside you. And when payday comes, you have this one chance to release all that stress. Some people go binge shopping, buying luxury items that they feel they deserve. Some people have a binge of alcohol and a lot of partying. Some people buy things at whim such as a car or an appliance or some subscription. You just feel so tired that when there is an opportunity to release, you grab the chance. It's not wrong to release your stress, to treat yourself once in a while. But often times, we get carried away with our spending. You feel excited when you get to a sale that before you know it, your cart is full of things you really don't need. You feel entitled to luxury items because you worked hard for it. Understandable. But all your savings are wiped out for that one moment of happiness that you feel you deserve. This is bad financial decision-making.

Another pitfall most people fall into is the circular pit of debt. Credit can be very tempting, with a lot of banks offering promos and enticing perks to goad you to avail. Because you have the assurance of a salary, you become confident about using your credit card. You know that at the end of the day, all your bills are going to be taken care of by your employer anyway. But at the end of the month, some of your purchases go beyond your limit and you acquire debts. Over time, these debts pile up. Small debts may not seem significant. But compounded over a long time, these small debts can actually cripple you for life. Before you know it, you are working only to pay your debts. Even your retirement can be sucked dry by these loan schemes.

How do we escape this trap? Perhaps the young Carlos Slim Helu can help us out. Discipline is what we need. We need to master ourselves and our inclinations. You have to examine your life, from your purchases, your properties, to all the things that you own. Ask yourself, "Do I really need this? Can I live without it? Is it bringing me closer to my dream?" This is not an easy question because we tend to justify ourselves. But we are only fooling ourselves if we are not able to sift through what we really need and what are just some things that we want. If you want to be rid of debt, live within your means. If you want to keep your savings, buy only what is necessary. I am not saying that we should be Scrooges and deny ourselves some luxury. We do need to be happy at times. Cheat days are there to help us go through the month. But the point I am emphasizing is that there is a greater purpose to disciplining yourself than just not being happy. You are saving up because there is a purpose you want to spend that money for later on.

Examine your life once again. Take out the things you don't really need. Living a simple life is actually possible and even enjoyable. You will realize that you can actually live in your own house. Commuting may not be that bad if you are near train stations. Buying in bulk can actually be more practical than buying single items. Simple things taken together have great impact. Master your natural inclinations so you can be financially free from all the debtors, loan schemes and addictive behaviors that have prevented you from living the life you truly deserve.

Chapter 2: What Do You Need to Be Financially Free

If we are going to study the mind of any billionaire, we cannot miss to pick the mind of Jeff Bezos, the founder of Amazon, the world's largest online retail distributor. He is currently number 1 in Forbes richest persons of 2019 with a net value of $150 billion. With a computer science and electrical engineering background, Jeff started out in a number of technology and banking firms before he ventured on his own. He could have been satisfied with the high-paying jobs at Fitel and Banker's Trust but he knew he was meant for greater things. With his savings and an extra boost from his parents, Jeff formed an online bookstore and named it Amazon. The website steadily garnered following and eventually overtook his competitors. But Jeff was still not satisfied. He pushed his online shop from books and ventured into music and videos. With steady traction, Amazon went to cover a lot of retail goods including grocery items. Today, Amazon solidifies its position in the Americas as the dominant online retailer, and looking to expand to India.

Back in his university studies, Jeff was very active and became president of the Students for the Exploration and Development of Space in Princeton University. Outer space totally fascinated Jeff. He dreamed of exploring extraterritorial landscapes, dreaming of turning them into theme parks someday. Perhaps it is this craziness or perhaps, visionary spirit, that fueled Jeff to reimagine the way we consume. Instead of conforming to the usual, Jeff looks to the skies and sees an expansion of possibilities. In a speech, Jeff Bezos says "The common question that gets asked in business is 'Why? That's a good question, but an equally valid question is, 'why not?'"

We may not have schooled in Princeton and gotten summa cum laude as Jeff did. We may not have his starting capital as he pushed for his online store. We may not have the same networks as he had. But one thing we can learn from this visionary is the mindset of seeing possibilities. If you want to be truly financially free, you must also have the same optimism as Jeff has on seeing things differently. Instead of clinging to the usual and to the conventional, those who succeed in life are able to destroy the boxes that limit them.

Pushing boundaries means reimagining what we can do beyond what we usually do. The norm is the capitalist-employee system we are currently chained to. This is what pays the bills and affords us some luxury. Is there something beyond this system that will also pay the bill and afford us more luxury? Can we see possibilities in the everyday life we lead?

There have been a number of visionaries who have reimagined the world and created small fortunes for themselves. Spotify for example democratized music to be affordable and accessible to anyone, making the listening experience more intimate. Uber and Lyft have revolutionized ride-sharing experiences, bypassing the difficulty of hailing cabs and commuting. Google Maps has made satellites a common possession. Apple has paved the way for enhancing communication in a multisensory manner. With technology, obscure individuals could build a fortune by tapping into a niche yet unexplored.

And you could do the same. Look at the world around you. Is there a way that you can rethink how people do things to make it faster, easier, more convenient, more accessible, cheaper or just plain better? Is there a problem in your community that you can think of a better solution to? Start from your own house. Can you think of a better way to cook meals healthier or in a more convenient way? Is there a better solution to dirty floor than manually scrubbing it on your knees? In your family, is there a way to keep you all interacting in spite of being physically apart? Are there ways to make your children safe while you work? Move away to your neighborhood. Is there a better solution to garbage than a truck collecting from house to house? Can schools be more inclusive of other races and ethnicities? Is there a way to erase traffic completely? Go to a national level or even cross the international. Is there space for a universal market of goods so that you can buy corn from Peru while you are in Europe? Can I tour the Louvre from the comfort of my desk? Is there a way to entice poor people to avail of insurance and investments? There are endless problems around you that are waiting to be solved. There are a lot of materials in your very area that may inspire you to create the next great product. The call of success demands that we innovate. Jeff Bezos puts it more dramatically when he says "Innovate or die."

But being expansive about your imagination entails risks and consequences. Jeff's wager on Amazon paid off, but he didn't know it would be a success until it did. There are a lot of inventions and ideas that have reached initial stages of execution but died before they could be fully realized. You will surely commit mistakes on your first, your second, your third, and your nth try. But billionaires like Jeff Bezos would only see these mistakes as necessary steps in order to fulfill your dreams. It is not risk free after all, and so you are asked to be courageous enough to try. Without even trying, then no change is possible. If you are only going to listen to your own self-criticisms, the idea dies without bearing fruit. If you listen to others doubt, then you have allowed them to succeed in robbing you of the wealth you deserve.

It is very scary to try something new. If you have been used to doing something for all of your life, doing something different is horrifying. Dying your hair orange will be unimaginable to someone who has had black hair all of her life. Transferring schools or homes are always traumatizing. Our bodies resist change because it naturally longs for the predictable, the usual, and the known. We feel a sense of peace when we are able to do things are usual way, taste the pancakes we have been accustomed to, drive the usual byways, watch the same formulaic movies, buy the same quality of products we've known. We are programmed to expect the expected.

But if we choose to stay where we are comfortable, isn't this also as horrifying, as traumatizing? It may be so wonderful to remain adolescents forever without any responsibilities. But imagine being adolescents forever? The mark of maturity is the capacity to change, to adapt and to innovate. What is important is the mindset of possibility. Without this mindset, then you remain chained to your desk, typing away in some obscure office, happily ignorant of the wealth you could possibly have. To open yourself to possibilities is not just rewarding financially, but holistically too. We begin to have a sense of greater meaning when we can feel that we are growing from our comfort zones.

Chapter 3: Finding Your Why

You may not know him, but you may constantly be using his products. Larry Page, one of the founders of Google, along with Sergey Brin, is valued at $55.8 billion, the tenth richest man in Forbes for 2019. Together with Brin, they have managed to make information organized and accessible. Their background in computer science and the desire for building a more superior search engine fueled the quest to build Google. What started from a PhD dissertation in Stanford University became the world's most popular and biggest search engine, capable of processing trillions of data in milliseconds, accessible from all parts of the world. And they are far from stopping as Google continues to explore the boundaries of searching, venturing into democratizing all forms of knowledge from map making to personal mail messaging.

What makes Page and Brin successful? What drives these two in the millions of people they have inspired to be the success Google is right now? In an interview, Larry Page says, "If we were motivated by money, we would have sold the company a long time ago and ended up on a beach." They could have stopped and sold the rights to the PageBank algorithm they first developed and became settled into their retirements. That program alone would have sold for billions of dollars. But Page and Brin persisted with their idea. Instead of buying out their company, they proceeded to develop it, pushing it to its limits and exploring all that it was capable of. They were not satisfied with just getting filthy rich. In fact, money was not their motivation. Page says "Sergey and I founded Google because we're super optimistic about the potential for technology to make the world a better place." They are not buying out

Google and selling it to the next richest person precisely because they are not after the money. They are motivated by that desire to make the world a better place by providing accessible information.

Motivation. This is a key ingredient in the success of the world's richest people. They have a goal that makes them get out of the morning, burn long hours inventing and researching, go hungry over projects, battle criticisms and challenges and push beyond their successes. The goal is not a hobby they can return to only if they are merely interested or have the time. The goal consumes them that they spend every waking minute working towards achieving it. If you were to be financially free, then we must have motivation.

The question then is, "What motivates you?" This is probably one of the most difficult questions we can ask ourselves. Young people especially may not have a clue what they want to do in life. Without posing this question, we run the risk of simply jumping on to one opening to the next. There must be a space and time where we can be alone and ask ourselves "What is it that I truly want? What is my goal in life?"

It does not matter if you have the answer right now. Many people may still be searching for it well into their retirement years. But the more important than having the exact answer is the posing of the question. We must learn to ask this question every day to help us in our journey towards financial freedom.

If your goal in life is only to make money, then a paycheck lifestyle will suit you. Having the dependability of a salary might be enough to keep you going to your office and enduring the long hours so you can pay your bills and enjoy some luxury. If you only desire a modest income, just enough to eke out a living and sustain your family, then having a regular job is appropriate. There is nothing wrong with this especially if you believe in it fully.

But if you go beyond money, then a paycheck lifestyle will not be enough for you. Page and Brin never thought about settling in only for the money.

They had a problem they want to solve: "how do we make information accessible to everyone?" They realize quickly that money is not the goal in life; it merely comes when you are working towards a greater goal. Making the world a better place is a higher goal than just making money. With bigger goals come bigger rewards as the Google founders have experienced. And this is also true in our own simple lives. When we desire to be financially free, we cannot make money as the end point and goal. Money is only the means to the end which we desire most. It is one among many tools we need in order to achieve our goals. The money will also come when we are working towards our goals. And there is greater fulfilment when we achieve our goals rather than focusing on the tools.

So we return to that question, "What is my goal? What is it that I want to do and accomplish most in life? What is that problem I want to solve? What is my passion?" Take time to pose this question. Work towards having some answers to it. But if we ask this on an everyday basis, we may realize that some motivations are only temporary and fleeting. Today, you may say that I want to have a degree. When you get it, then you ask yourself, what now? Motivations have to be separate from mere wants or hobbies. A true motivation must be something you think you can give your whole life to. Another way of phrasing it is to ask "What can I see myself doing for the rest of my life?" If you find that your current job may not be answering that question, then reconsider. Align your life in such a way that you are accomplishing that which you are most motivated to.

Motivation can be found in your interests and talents. Are you interested in computers and technology? Are you good at drawing or acting? Does Mathematics come easy to you? Does speaking in front of a crowd interest you? We must never stop discovering what interests are, what are strengths may be. You may even surprise yourself that you are actually good at some things only when you begin trying them out. Does a photography career suit your temperament? Are you more alive when you are dealing with sick people? Find that which you are passionate about and turn that, not just into a hobby, but a lifestyle which you can actually live on.

You can also start finding motivation in your weakness and vulnerabilities. You may not be good in driving for example. If you create a blog about that, sharing your weakness, people may be drawn to you and start subscribing to your blog. When you know your weakness, you can quickly exploit that to become your strength. There are a lot of business which thrive on finding people's needs and meeting them there in order to find common solutions. Page and Larry may not know art the way people with art degrees do. But they have created a program that will allow you to have as much information as you can about art, turning you into an instant master in a few clicks. Your vulnerabilities can be strengths as well.

Finally, we the more important question to ask is "What keeps you motivated?" It may not be enough to know what you want. The problem is if you can sustain that motivation when the hype is over, when there are problems encountered, when the honeymoon phase finishes. We will talk more about sustaining this motivation, but in this chapter's discussion of motivation, it is important to remind us that our motivations need to have some sense of stability and permanency. Find your motivation and stay motivated.

Chapter 4: Characteristics to Prevent Procrastination

If there was one thing that summed up the technocrat Larry Ellison, it would be 'relentless'. He encountered a lot of challenges as he struggled to keep Oracle Corporation on top of the database industry. He encountered a lot of competition from other database systems such as Sybase, Informix and Microsoft. He battled a lot of critics who challenged his views on the direction of Oracle and the people who should be in position. But he managed to still push his perspectives and rally Oracle to be at the top of its game. He is currently the 6th wealthiest person in the world according to Forbes for the year 2019.

Relentlessness. The indefatigability in pursuing your goals. Relentlessness is a value that we should also inculcate if we are to attain financial freedom. Relentlessness can be summed in two important characteristics. The first is consistency and the second is persistence. These two terms are often used interchangeably by many. They are related but they are not necessarily the same. They both are needed to help us accomplish our objectives and goals in life, yet they represent two distinct values which have their own guiding principles and skill sets. We will break up these two characteristics and their implication on financial freedom.

Consistency refers to how often you can replicate a particular action. When you are shooting a target, you are told that you are consistent if you keep on hitting the same spot over and over again. When you hit the bull's eye one out of ten times, then you are just lucky, not necessarily consistent. But if you hit the bull's eye ten out of ten times, then luck has nothing to do with your success. You are simply consistently skilled.

In the very same way, our approach to success must not be a one-shot deal. When you are able to do an excellent presentation, you cannot say that you are an expert if the next one is pretty bad. Your output is not taken into singular moments of excellence, but evaluated across time. As the term implies, you have to replicate your success. In order to be perceived as a good salesman, you must be able to convince not just one customer, but a lot of customers, over and over again. The numbers game will provide an objective measure of how much you are able to replicate your success. If your sales are far and between, you have to reconsider your skills and strategies. One good client is not a success; it is lucky break. In business, we don't like lucky breaks. We need consistent good breaks. We need successful habits.

Let us break down in what happens when we form a habit from a cognitive perspective. For example, you want to be excellent at shooting a ball.

So you take the ball, aim for the ring, and shoot it. It will take many tries before you are able to shoot one. But when you are able to do so for the first time, your brain will take note of the position you took which allowed you to shoot the ball. It will try to remember the angle of the shot, the power used in the release, the muscles involved in the perfect shot. Your brain and your body will try to replicate the form until it is able to do it another time. If you do it again, the muscles involved with moving remember that position. When you do it another time, the muscle memory is reinforced. Brain circuits controlling that particular muscle group are also reinforced. The more you use it, the more the brain remembers. Through time, even without conscious effort, your brain and your body will shoot that ball on target.

In the very same way, when we are trying to form successful habits, you need to do it over and over again. When you are trying to sell a product, you have to try it a first time and see what went wrong and what went right. You try to evaluate the things that have led to your first sale and you try to replicate it. You try another customer and apply the same principle. You do it to another and another, until the script is ingrained in your memory. After a while, you will be able to hit that sale like a machine. If you want to learn how to learn digital art you can sell online, you have to keep on creating and drawing every day without fail. The everyday practice will strengthen your mind and your muscles so that you are able to replicate your successes.

The opposite process of forgetting works in the same way. If you don't keep on using a particular part of your body, it atrophies. If you don't keep on doing the same action, you will tend to forget it. If you are not engaged in selling in an everyday basis, you will forget how to market a product or engage customers. If you miss one day of not drawing or creating, your learning is impeded and the progress becomes stagnated. The secret to habit forming is that if you do it every day no matter how you are feeling. There are days when you want to quit and have a cheat day. Don't. When you feel that you want to stop, motivate yourself that today's attempt will be the last. You just keep on plodding on and on, until you are able to master your craft. Only then can you attain consistency in your work.

The other value is persistence. This refers to our capacity to try again. Returning to the arrow analogy, when you don't hit a target, persistence is seen when you try again. No matter how many times you fail to hit the target, a persistent person is one who will not quit. Consistency refers to the objective replication of results. Persistence is objective desire to achieve your goals. If consistency deals with the brain and the body, persistence focuses mainly on the heart. The will to succeed is the essence of persistence.

Persistence is needed in all aspects of life, whether you are starting a business, engaging in a relationship, working towards some goal. The general assumption to all effort is that we are limited. In whatever we do, we will always encounter problems. We will have our bad days, moments when we are down and not in the mood, or terribly affected by personal news. We will have our vulnerabilities, skills we may not have yet perfected, new concepts we haven't mastered. As humans, we have our own limitations.

Persistence recognizes those limitations. A persistent person is not one who will say that they are perfect, that they are invulnerable. There is such an honesty in a persistent person to be aware of their limitation. But this does not define them. Yes, there is a limitation. But there is also a limitless capacity to change and to try again. The persistent person knows that there is a second chance. And they set aside all their limitations and try to go beyond that, attempting another time until they succeed. Persistence is trying over and over again, regardless of the results. In the end, success is achieved through relentless persistence.

In the end, we both need consistency and persistence in achieving our goals. Without consistency, we will not be able to replicate the targets we have set for ourselves. Without persistence, we may be disheartened to try again. We need both the brain and the heart working together to achieve that which we want to accomplish. Many people get disheartened quickly with small failures. If an investment becomes bust, we let the failure set in for a long time, even doubting our own capacities and talents. If we hear criticism from people about the product we are selling, we may feel insecure and react defensively or even walk away from the issue. Doubt and insecurity are our main enemies when we strive for financial freedom. When we entertain doubt and insecurity, we are refusing to believe that we have a capacity to go beyond our limits. Yes, we fail. But we are also capable of trying again. If we are going anywhere near the status of these billionaires, we cannot let simple challenges deter us from the financial freedom we deserve. Make success a habit. Try, then try again.

Chapter 5: How Far Can You Visualize?

The power of visualization is important to achieve when we want to accomplish anything. The capacity to see beyond is a potential few of us have maximized. Yet, these billionaires show us consistently how a vision aligns our everyday action to the goal we want to achieve. With a clear vision of what we want, we are able to direct all our actions into attaining it. Without any vision at all, your efforts can be spontaneous and direction-less, leading to wasted energies and efforts. And some people do operate in this vision-less way. They enter a company not knowing what to expect and clueless as to what they really want to achieve. They end up forty years as employees still without much direction into their retirement. There is a sense of loss when you think of all the efforts and resources that have been expended all for a disorganized or even missing purpose.

It is not actually easy to visualize what you want to do or be. Many people can function without much vision for a good number of years. Perhaps the process is too tedious or complicated they don't even bother to try. But it is possible. There are ways to visualize a goal you want to set for yourself. I will provide you with a short exercise that will help you achieve this.

First, take some time out during the day to be alone and silent. The environment has a lot of stimuli which may distract you from listening to yourself. In 24 hours, you are surrounded by many noises that you fail to hear your own. You end up simply listening and eventually following the loudest voice, not knowing that it may not be for you. So take time out to be silent and alone. Close your eyes to shut out all the distractions and simply focus on your breathing. Breathe in, breathe out. Breathe in, breathe out. Breathe in, breathe out.

Breathe in positivity, breath out negativity. Breathe in, breathe out.

Next, ask yourself the following. Be honest as you can. You may not have the answers now, but just start posing those questions to yourself.

- Can I see myself achieving my goal?
- How do I look like? If my goal is to have my own house, how do I see that house? What are the details of this vision?
- Who are the people around me as I reach my desired end? Who am I surrounded with? How do they feel as I achieve my dreams?
- How do I feel as I accomplish my goal?

This exercise asks you to visualize yourself accomplishing your goal. You have to be very vivid as to how you look, feel, think when you have achieved your goal. How happy are you when you have amassed that target wealth? Who are the people surrounding you at this point? What does it feel like to have achieved your goals in life?

The power of attraction says that if you can see it, it will happen. If you think that it is going to be true, then it will be true. If you think that you will fail, then you will fail. This principle also applies to visioning. We use this exercise to attract the universe to conspire to make our dreams become a reality. You have to see it so your dream will materialize. If you desire a brand new car, think of it everyday, see it in your imagination, and then one day, it will be yours. If you desire yourself as owning the company you work in, imagine that you are that person. Imagine you in your best suit, working in that prestigious office, being served by your employees and talking to big clients. Visualize it and it will be true.

The converse is also true. If you are a pessimist and you think that you will fail, then you will really fail. Self-fulfilling prophecies already condition your mind and that bends the context according to how you visualize things. If you think that you will not be promoted this year, then you will not be promoted. You may get jitters when you are preparing for an interview and you think that you will not be accepted. You will predispose yourself to fail and you will not get accepted. Take away those negative thoughts and simply focus on achieving your goal.

Do this exercise every day and you will see how motivated you can be. Even if you encounter down moments or when you hear criticism, you have to anchor that to the one vision that you have. It will make the worst days bearable knowing that it will all pass. You are also able to celebrate milestones because they remind you that you are approaching nearer your goal. Practice visioning every day and you can turn your goals into reality.

Chapter 6: 3 Friends You Should Hang Out With

Much is unknown about the billionaire Amancio Ortega. He has rarely given interviews or appeared in public limelight. He leads a very introverted life, away from media, away from the fanfare common to those who are rich and famous. His is a quiet kind of leadership, steering his flag line Zara and the Inditex fashion group to become one of the most recognized brand in fashion. His work speaks well for him as he claims the fifth spot on the Forbes 2019 richest persons, being the second wealthiest European after Bernard Arnault and the wealthiest retailer.

The secret to Ortega's success came from destroying the old mold of the fashion industry. He started out working when he was 14 as a shop hand in a local shirt store called Gala. Learning the tricks of the trade, he began to sell quilted bathrobes. This sold well and he moved on selling fashionable clothes for women. He founded the fast fashion movement, then an unheard of concept in fashion. Before, designers would dictate what people should be wearing and enticing them to buy them after fashion shows. But Ortega did the opposite. He went to the people and asked them what they wanted to wear, producing their clothes in an instant. His running stocks were always changing as the type of clothes people wanted to wear changed. He kept on listening to people's tastes and suited his business to cater to them. This proved successful as Ortega began amassing different fashion retail stores like Massimo Dutti, Oysho, Tempe, Stradivarius, Pull and Bear, and Bershka.

But in spite of his wealth, Ortega remains humble. He still goes to the cafeteria, lining up with the rest of the employees. He would often be seen talking to ordinary workers as though he wasn't any different from any of them. He does not wear a suit to work, preferring a simple polo. He knew his employees and kept on bouncing ideas with them. He even said, "Store employees have the best understanding of... customer tastes."

Amancio Ortega's example shows us that even the wealthiest people have a lot to learn from even the simplest of people. They are able to network from all social classes rather than sticking to their own. And this is something that we can also emulate. We can even push Ortega's classy example to a more expansive networking scheme. We may attain financial freedom easier if we are to practice the 360 networking.

The 360 networking principle is borrowed from the 360 feedback concept in human resource studies. In terms of management, the 360 feedback is used as a standard method of giving feedback to an employee. As the name implies, a person is given feedback from a number of people surrounding him. The first group are those below him in terms of rank, the second are his peers and the third are his direct supervisors and bosses. Feedback is given by all these three groups so the person has a better picture of his performance. This is a more superior approach to feedback giving compared to previous models which have relied on only one view of a person. By using a 360 feedback approach, human resource management can be more objective and holistic in evaluating employees.

In terms of financial freedom, the 360 feedback concept can be expanded to the 360 networking approach. Like the feedback model, the 360 networking principle works by classifying people into three groups: those below your social level, those within your social circle and level and those above your standing. By fostering and strengthening these social ties, you are able to learn a lot from different people as well as gain their trust and friendship. This may even be used in terms of business networking, where you are able to cast a wider client base when you surround yourself with different classes of people. We will now discuss the importance of being with these three different group.

First, you have to surround yourself with those below your social level. You can be pretty honest about your social status and can identify people who may above or below you. There is great value then in keeping your connections to them intact. If you are an employee, be sure that you know the maintenance personnel or guards in your office. If you are a boss, immerse yourself with your employees. There is a lot to learn from them that you may not necessarily know. Ortega knew the value of this when he would sit with his employees. Being the boss may not allow him to really see his customers on the ground. By talking to his employees, he is able to know what his market wants, how do they think, what will interest them to buy. When he talks with them, he uses their languages because in this way, he is able to win their trust and friendship. These interactions provide him with the necessary information and social network with which to funnel his next great fashion line. His clothes sell because they speak to people. So being with those below your social level is not condescending or patronizing. You do not relate to them simply because you pity them. You remain close to them because there is a lot of learnings you can get from interacting with them.

Jeff Bezos of Amazon also holds that principle. He says that in Amazon, any employee has the right to be heard especially if her insight is something unique and irrefutable by those above him. It may just be an accident in life that you have different social classes. But knowledge knows no classes and may be found in the seemingly simplest of people. A great idea is still a great idea, regardless of the social class of who thought of it first.

The second class of people you ought to surround yourself are your peers, those in the same social class as you. In one sense, you know each other better because you have the similar backgrounds, similar upbringings, similar cultures and perhaps similar ways of thinking. A designer may bounce off ideas with another designer because they have a shared knowledge, passions and concerns about design. A fellow manager may be easier to share concerns to because they know how it is to handle people and deadlines. A sense of camaraderie and sharing of knowledge and resources is built by associating yourself with people of your same class.

But being with people in the same class also opens up the possibility of competition. We really never outgrow childhood competition especially those we grew up with. Because people in the same class do similar things, they may also at the same time be competitors of each other. Some designers are contemporaries and don't talk to each other for fear of pirating ideas. The competition should not hinder you from socializing with them. The more that you are competing with them, the more that you should befriend them. A healthy competition actually boosts productivity. You are more motivated to succeed and work harder because you know there is someone out there who can beat you at your game. The point of a competition is to raise the standard of quality and service of your products all to benefit your customers. If you simply have a monopoly, then productivity can stagnate as there is no impulse to change. Jeff Bezos' Amazon in the United States has a competition in Jack Ma's Alibaba in China. A Ford will compete well with a Volkswagen. Microsoft persistently battles out with Oracle. Apple will see competition from Samsung or Huawei or Nokia. All of these competitions only seek to drive people to be better at what they do.

The final group that you have to surround yourself with are those above you. Some sense of social climbing is needed to motivate you to eventually be in their level. As with those below you, there is a lot to learn from supervisors, bosses, mentors who have a greater wealth of experience and knowledge from us. They may have a broader perspective than we do because they have been past what we are currently experiencing. They may even see the bigger picture in the company we work for that can give us the perspective we need. Do not be shy to engage with your bosses. Some people find it awkward to talk with their bosses on a friendly level, thinking that this is sucking up to them. There is a lot to learn simply by being with people who are more experienced than you or belong to social classes you would want to belong to. Ask questions from them and you will see how eager they are to impart knowledge. Older people especially are finding ways they can teach their craft and learnings to the next generation. Take the initiative and start a conversation. You can only benefit from such interactions.

The power of networking lies in casting wide social nets. These networks provide you with a bigger resource than just sticking to one. Foster connections with everyone around you because you can learn from anybody if you keep an open mind. You may also need this social networks when you want to improve what you are currently doing. You can seek advice from your bosses on what to do next. You can listen to bystanders and what interests them so you could be inspired to turn their interests to businesses. Sound off with peers and welcome the completion. A 360 network principle will allow you to cast wider and wider nets of influence that you can use to your advantage.

Chapter 7: Different Ways to Earn Passive Income

The French billionaire Bernard Arnault built his empire by steadily acquiring a variety of businesses. He started with construction company and turned it into a real estate business. He developed a chain holiday accommodations next. The crown of his business was obtained when he acquired Financiere Agache, a luxury goods company. He also managed business in the textile industry, retail wears, a diaper manufacturing company, a newspaper, perfume business, webpages, supermarket chains, and a yacht business among others. All of these booming businesses have turned Bernard Arnault into the richest European and third richest person in the world as of 2019.

Though Arnault is more known for his luxury brand items such as Louis Vuitton, he has expanded his sources of income to cover a variety of industries. In business, this is called diversification, wherein you distribute your investments across various, and not necessarily related businesses. The advantage to this is that you have different sources of income. Each one is earning and competing in a different market from each other. Diversification will also mitigate risks. When you distribute your investments, you distribute the risks of your investments and become less affected when there are fluctuations in a particular market. We can learn from this approach from Arnault. We may not have a luxury goods business like him, but we can learn from his constant resourcefulness in spreading his investments.

We can apply this in our situation when we look for other possible sources of income aside from your main line of work. Part of financial freedom is to extend minimal effort with more return. This means that a successful business venture is one where your profits far outweigh the amount of work you put in. Imagine that with minimal effort, you are receiving so much more. This is actually possible when we talk about passive income. This financial concept refers to the inflow of money with minimal active effort. Active effort is when you are getting paid for some output you produce, which may be project-based or fixed income. When you create a video for an employer, your fee is an active cash flow. When you work in an office with a regular paycheck, you have an active cash flow.

On the other hand, passive income is making money work for you. Akin to investment, a passive source of income will allow you to still receive money without much effort. But you have to take note that this should not be your main work yet. This is a pitfall some people become trapped in, thinking that they can simply rely on alternate sources of income immediately. Passive incomes take time to bear fruit. Some will even require a start-up capital. But all of these will need to take some time before they can start earning for you. So never replace your active with your passive income right away. The passive income should only augment or add to your active income in the beginning. I will give you some ideas in the next chapter on how to grow your passive income.

What are some of these passive income resources? It will take some imagination for you to see how with so little effort, you can actually make money. But you would be surprised that some of these schemes turn out to be substantial money-makers. Here are some ways you can explore as passive income resources:

Blogging

Do you have a passion for writing? Do you have a knack for taking pictures or creating digital art? You can easily turn this into cash through blogging. There are many do-it-your own blog sites that are found on the Internet, some of them for free. You can write anything and everything under the sun that you find an interest on. Like a modern diary, a blog can help chronicle and organize your thoughts in a digital format.

To turn a simple blog into a cash cow, you have to make sure that you are interesting enough to be read. You need to create a lot of traffic of readers, drawing people into your website. This will mean that you should choose a niche topic for your blog. Instead of writing anything and everything under the sun, focus on one general topic that you are familiar with or you think a lot of people will have an interest on. There are many blogs on fashion, cosmetics, video games, arts and crafts, technology and sports and entertainment. To be strategic about it, you can choose a topic that nobody else is talking about so you could be the pioneer blog. If you choose a common topic, you have to be exceptionally good at it or offer something unique.

Keep your content always fresh and entertaining. Make sure that the material will make your audience want for more. For example, a blog on sports should cover news on the latest sporting events, analysis of players and games and even statistics and team standings on popular sports. A blog reviewing food recipes should constantly feature a new dish or a signature dish of well-known people. The materials should come in at a regular interval so that people will look forward to your next post. Don't just post when you want to or when you have an idea. If the interval is only upon your whim, there may be long periods between posts and that may throw people off. People want to feel that your blog is alive so make sure that your posting is regular.

When you have gained enough readership, your blog will attract advertisements. Companies might approach you if they could attach ads to your blog entries. This is where your passive income comes in. As long as your blog is interesting and generates a lot of traffic, advertisers will always be attracted to invest in you. Just imagine you are getting paid for writing posts that you are passionate about with zero starting capital.

Vlogging

The concept of vlogging is similar to blogging, except with videos. This is gaining more popularity as the people are more attracted to audio-visual stimuli. People will view your blog more if there is a multi-sensory experience. Instead of writing about how to put on different cosmetic products, just show how it is done. Instead of listing a recipe, show the ingredients and demonstrate how to cook a particular cuisine. You will still get paid via advertisements if you have generated a lot of traffic. If you are a popular vlogger, companies will even pay you to feature their products on your videos. You get free products, you earn money while you just enjoy doing what you do.

In order to be good at vlogging, it may be strategic to invest on a good camera. An inexpensive one will do provided you have clear images. You might also need to learn some camera editing skills, knowing how to create shots, splice segments and create a flow to your videos. If you aren't ready for this, you can always hire a professional video editor to handle the technical aspects. Sound and video effects may even be added to highlight aspects of your videos. But your videos must have high quality. No matter how good your content is, if the video aspect is not well-made, it will simply be ignored.

Vlogging can even be used to promote your own products. Start-ups usually use home-made videos to advertise their own products. If you don't have a big capital to advertise on mainstream channels, vlogging is the cheapest and most effective medium of advertising. And in vlogging, more than the product itself, people are interested on the vlogger himself. The personality of the vlogger is infused into the product. If you are funny or quirky, if you have strong opinions or weird mannerisms, if you have a sexy accent or you interview guests well, people will be tuned. In vlogging, you have to sell the product with your personality.

Again, the same principle with blogging holds for vlogging. Make sure that your material is good, fresh and on-point. People nowadays rarely watch long videos, so make sure that your clips are short and direct. Apply appropriate audio-visuals that will accompany your story. Keep the posts regular so people will anticipate for your every release. Monetize your vlog by inviting companies to advertise on your site. Use social media to gain extensive networks and varied followers. Communicate with your viewers so the interaction becomes real-time. The more real you are to the viewers, the more real the experience is, then the more people will view you.

Affiliate Marketing

To understand how you and companies actually earn from these online advertisements, we have to learn the concept of affiliate marketing. This is a tool used by companies to use local influencers to market their products for a price. For a company, this would mean advertising on popular bloggers to reach the audiences being catered to by these influencers. For bloggers, this means increasing their passive income while showcasing their passion.

Take blogging and vlogging. If you have a regular channel or a website of your own that generates high traffic, advertisers will contact you if they can advertise in your site. This may be in the form of banners or headers along your page, or a link box in one of your pages. Companies pay you to put these links in your page. When anybody reading your blog or viewing your site clicks on the website that is called a lead. With one click, you have led your viewers to the advertiser's page. If the viewer buys that product eventually, that is called a sale. Companies will pay you depending on the number of leads you have generated and how much of those have turned into actual sales. Companies will have a breakdown of the commission you have for each lead and sales. In effect, as bloggers and vloggers, you have become the platform in which these companies reach the audience they ordinarily cannot access.

To be good at affiliate marketing, you should generate a lot of traffic. This means being perceived as an expert in the area of interest you are exploiting. If people see you have credibility reviewing products, then they would be more enticed to buy these via your advertisers' sites. If companies perceive you as having a broad market, then they would be more attracted to partner with you. So create a good image for yourself as a credible influencer. The cash will simply flow if you play your cards well.

Digital assets

When you log on to the Internet, every aspect of a given page is a digital asset. From the icons, to the font, to the photos, documents and videos, digital assets cover everything that can be stored digitally. Advertisers rely heavily on the use of these assets when promoting their products. For example, you want to promote a brand new watch, you have to use photos that will showcase your products. That photo is an asset. If you want to promote a new car and you will use a jingle, that song or sound is a digital asset. Each asset must be unique and distinct from each other.

How can you monetize digital assets? Companies buy digital assets. If you create an icon, you have to register that and get a license. Companies will have to pay you to use your icon in their webpage. If you are any good at digital arts, this would be a good source of income. If you like creating catchy jingles or inventing quirky fonts, you can earn a lot. If many companies from all over the world use your digital asset, all of that would mean cash flow to you. Just be careful about copyright issues. Have your digital asset licensed so have a legal claim on your product. There are some who use stock photos without permission and that means an infringement on licensing privileges. License your art and get paid for what you love doing.

These are just some of the ways that you can earn passive income. It doesn't mean putting totally no effort at all on making a blog or creating an asset.

There is some creativity and resources used in making your products. But once you put them out on the market, you may not have to monitor these actively. Income will start to flow without you minding your vlog on an hourly basis. The more you create, the more income will come in. Be sure to have the legal documents for your website items so you have a claim in case of copyright issues. Technology is fast expanding and you wouldn't want to miss out on the cash flow that comes with democratizing influence. Even simple people can have a slice of their own passive income fortune.

Chapter 8: Different Ways to Invest Your Money

The third wealthiest person in the world believes in the power of investments. Warren Buffet, chairman and CEO of Berkshire Hathaway, learned about investments early on in school when he would hang around a regional stock brokerage firm near his father's office. When he was 11 years old, he bought his first three shares on Cities Service. Before graduating from college, he had amassed $9,800 through his investments and businesses. Warren Buffet is the living testimony on the power of the Stock Exchange to amass wealth on an exponential level.

Investing takes passive income a step higher. Again, this will not be your main source of living immediately as it will take some time to establish a presence and earn. But the rewards for this may actually surpass your active income. There is a lot of risk involved in investments. So you must do a lot of research when you begin investing. Don't jump into an investment you may not know personally. A lot of people will egg you to put your hard-earned money on a fast investment, only to end up in a scam. Study investment schemes and decide which ones suit your taste better. We will discuss some popular investment models which you can experiment on.

The general principle in investment is to buy low, sell high. Your profit increases if you buy an asset or an investment at a lower price and then sell it at a higher rate. Market prices will fluctuate so there is great need for timing when you will buy and sell investments. The market can also be very emotional. Prices can fluctuate rapidly due to various external and internal factors. As a buyer or a seller, you may be influenced by these fluctuations, leading you to costly decisions. Study markets well and you will succeed in these investment schemes.

High-yield savings account

The safest way to save your hard-earned money is to put it in a high yield savings account. Compared to a traditional saving account, high yield savings would yield 20 to 25 times more. There is less risk in a savings account because the money is not moving anywhere, it is just accumulating interest over the years. The earnings are proportional to the amount of capital you put in. The bigger the capital with a fixed interest, the higher return you will have. If you are retiring, your hard-earned money will slowly gain income if you deposit this on a savings account. The income return also increases in time. If you start saving at your 20's, by the time you reach your 60's, the interests have increased as your base money increases. Compare this to starting out saving at your 50's. With the same interest rate, the income return will be less because there is less time for the money to accumulate.

Though using a high-yield savings account is safe, this can also yield the lowest return. Since the money is just accumulating, there are less fluctuations but also less potential for your money to grow. If you are not the adventurous kind, then this kind of investment might be more suited for you. If you don't want to worry about putting your money or you are worried about market fluctuations, this may be for you. Just know that this will yield low returns compared to other investment schemes.

Index Funds

If you are feeling a little riskier, you may want to consider investing in index funds. This is an investing scheme that Warren Buffet recommended for those who are beginners in investing in the Stock Market. An index is a collection of companies listed in the stock market. Examples of this indices in the USA include Standard and Poor's 500 (S&P500), the Dow Jones Industrial Average and the Nasdaq 100. They cover a list of companies which may include big and small one, good and average performing accounts, and may add or delete companies. When you invest in an index fund, you are investing not one company alone, but on the entire set. You get the overall performance of all the companies in the index and that is how your investment will fare. If the overall performance is good, your investments may increase. If the market is doing poorly, you may have a lesser profit.

The index fund is suited for people who may not have the time, the interest, and the risk-taking appetite for investing in individual stocks. When you invest in an index fund, you only need to choose which index you feel is doing generally well. After that, you cannot mind your investment and proceed to busy yourself with other things. A fund manager will manage your account for you basing on the performance of the index you invested in. You don't need to worry about your investment on a daily basis. You don't need to be involved in the daily fluctuations of the market. You can simply monitor your investments every now and then. Indices rarely have drastic fluctuations because they are compounded as a whole. This investment is more appropriate for retirees who want to dabble in some stocks but don't have the time to micromanage.

With a less risky investment, you also have less return when you compare it to investing on individual stocks. Because indices do not fluctuate very much, the increase or decrease is small on a daily basis. Your stocks will not grow overnight. Instead, the gains will be more as you continue investing on that index for a longer period of time. There is a steady rise in your investment portfolio the market increases in size. If you are prepared to let your money stay in the market for a longer period of time, then index funds may be more apt for you.

Stocks

Investing in stocks have the highest risks but also the highest returns. The stock market may seem complicated to the beginner, but once you understand how it moves, it will be a very exciting challenge you can get hooked into. As with all investments, the stock market will work for under the principle of buying low and selling high. Buy a stock when the selling price is low or you think it is going to sell low. Sell a stock when you feel that the price is going to go down or when you are content with the profit you have gained. You hold a stock or you don't sell your stocks when you feel that the market is still moving, or you are waiting until your stocks have reached their optimum value before selling.

There are a lot of companies to choose from that have public stocks. You can choose from established companies or you may risk with upcoming companies. But you have to study the stock that you are going to invest in. Look at its history in the market. Is it generally increasing across the year? Does it peak at a particular time? Is it able to recover from losses? How high or low can its value reach? Is the company well-run? Are other people confident about its performance? Choose a stock that you trust and you feel that you have studied well.

The stock market is a very emotional arena. When people are afraid, they sell their stocks so they could protect their money. When they are confident, they will buy more stocks. The market may be predictable to some point, but not totally. It is dependent on a million factors including world events, political climates, oil prices, individual company performances, and the individual moods of people. Knowing this, you have to steel yourself when you invest in stocks. Don't panic immediately and sell your stocks when you feel that your stock is dipping. It is bound to bounce back soon after some time. On the other hand, don't keep on buying stocks that everyone else is buying because the price may fall off and you may be force to sell your stocks at a lower price. Don't be greedy. When you have attained a target profit, it is best to sell your stocks and get your profit. If you push it, you may incur a loss as well. Set limits also to how much money you are willing to lose. For example, you may opt to sell your stocks when you have breached 10% of your capital. These simple measures may protect your hard-earned investment, minimizing your losses and maximizing your profits.

Real Estate

If you find stocks too abstract, you might want to handle something more tangible like land. Real estate is one of the best kinds of investment because it will always increase in value. The value of real estate increases in time as the property and the surrounding area gets developed and demand increases. A land that you purchase today may increase in value by in just 5 years. Real estate presents one of the most stable investments you can buy.

Some people actually turn this into a business. The general rules of investment still remains when you deal with real estate. Buy estates at lower prices and sell them at higher values to increase your profit. When your location is strategic or if you have enhanced the area, you even have leverage to increase your selling price. You can also rent it out to receive cash flow every month. What's good with real estate is that it doesn't get affected by market fluctuations too much. It has a market of its own, as long as there is a demand for property. If you are the type that wants something tangible and safe, real estate can be a good match for you. When you compare it to investing in stocks, real estate provides a less risk for the investor. There are not enough studies to compare whether stocks or real estate provide the most profit across time. But you sure wouldn't lose if you invest in real estate. The only drawback to this is marketability. You have to be able to sell your property through good marketing. Study your property first so you can be credible as a seller. If you are not the marketing type, you can hire a broker to sell your property for you. But through time, you can develop skills that will allow you to be a charismatic real estate investor. You can proceed with buying more estates at the same time so you could increase your profits.

Chapter 9: How to Pass Your Wealth to Your Children

Born to a trading family, Mukesh Ambani started out in the textile business early. His father would involve him and his brother in the business, teaching them trade secrets and exposing them to the work. They live in a simple house in Mumbai and used the public transportation. Mukesh does not recall receiving an allowance but has fond memories of his father. He remembers, "My father shared with me his passion for business and entrepreneurship from very early on. Even when I was in high school, I used to spend long hours at the office on weekends." From then on, Mukesh Ambani gradually inherited the business and expanded beyond textiles to petrochemicals, telecommunication, and even sports. He is currently the richest man in Asia. All of these he attributes to his good upbringing in the family.

The mark of true success is not just measured with the attainment of financial wealth but also the capacity to pass that financial freedom to the next generation. As we have said earlier, financial freedom is not a one-shot lucky break; it is a habit that is developed through years and years of practice. People who get lucky in winning the lotto are not assured of gaining financial freedom. They may have the financial capital, but if they don't have the means to sustain it for themselves and for the next generation, then the funds are as quick to disappear. What we are emphasizing here is the necessity of teaching future generations how to be financially free so that the gains you have achieved in your lifetime are not put to waste.

In the first place, is there even a need to pass it forward to the next generation? Shouldn't we just be contented with gaining money in our lifetime? Well, if you plan to live forever, then passing it to others may not be such an issue. But as we accumulate more wealth, we realize that there must be a deeper reason why we do things. We may initially be doing it just to have more money. But as relational beings, we are moved to share with others those blessings we've received, most especially to our children. In fact, there is even greater potential for the next generation to accomplish more than the previous given proper training. They will start with a bigger capital, with more resources, and with the wealth of experience of their elders. There is more meaning then to why we strive to accumulate wealth when we know that our children will benefit from this.

But there have been a number of family business that have not succeeded. The parents have been very hard-working and industrious, expending all their efforts to maximize their investments. When their children take over, the business falls into mismanagement. Or some children may not even be interested in continuing the business. They may choose careers or directions far from what we want them to choose. We cannot say that financial freedom is a genetic trait that we pass on automatically to our children. The drive to succeed is not inherited immediately. The transition between generations will require more than assumptions. There must be a planned strategy on how to transfer not just the wealth, but the attitude that goes with the wealth.

So there is really great value in learning how to pass that financial freedom to the next generation in a systematic way. We include here a number of tips on how to inculcate that continuity so that your success becomes the success of the next generations. The goal is to multiply the wealth by empowering your family and your social networks, and not simply to pass things over.

Show them the ropes

If you want to make sure that the next generation succeeds in the way that you do, you have to show them the ropes. You have to involve your children in your work and not shut them out.

Commonly, parents try to work very hard in the office, earning money for their children. They go home tired and ask their children about school. The cycle repeats itself over and over. If this continues, there is really no way that one day they will want to do the kind of work that you do. The very first step is bridge that gap between work and home. Many self-help books will tell you to distinguish between work and home, never intermixing the two. This method works in for some aspects such as containing the negative pressure in the work and relaxing at home. But you can violate this rule if you think that the children will gain an interest in the kind of work that you do.

Do not underestimate the learning capability of children. Sure they may not be able to absorb everything all at once. They may find your work too technical and easily lose interest. You may be disappointed that they are not able to appreciate the work that you do. This is understandable and expected. But don't lose hope and give up. You expose them to your work, not to hire them as employees the next day, but to instill memories that they will not forget. If you are a tailor, bring them to the shop and have them try out cutting cloth. If you are a designer, bring your children to your workspace and explore coloring with them. If you are a banker, at least tour your children in your office. They will not get it at once. But they will remember that this is where their father or mother worked. When they grow up, they take these memories with them and influences the choices they will make for themselves.

Spoil versus deprive

There is a fine line between spoiling your children and depriving them. Both are extremes which we should avoid as parents. Spoiling children may have a tendency to develop privileged and dependent children. They know that their parents will provide everything for them so they have no motivation to try out things for themselves. If they find something difficult, they will simply turn to their parents who will always have the answers for them. Spoiling our children will make them weak and dependent on us. When the time comes for them to run the company or to choose a career for themselves, they feel helpless because they are not used to doing things on their own.

If you deprive them on the other hand, you risk traumatizing them. There have been many stories about children remember how their parents were too strict on them, even physically abusing they just to teach a lesson. Children crave affirmation and when their parents deprive them of that, they may have a tendency to distance themselves from you. The entire point then of engaging your children is lost if they feel estranged or afraid of you.

The difficult task we have as parents then is to strike a balance between these two extremes. The carrot and stick approach to influencing your children in a direction you want only works if you know when to use each instrument. Spoil them too much and they become needy. Deprive them too much and they will distance themselves from you.

Know how to use these two measures when you want to teach your children.

For example, if your children are doing well in their school, it may be good to reward them occasionally. The positive reinforcement works so they understand that doing well in school will lead to a reward. If they are bullying in school or they end up in some trouble, it may be good to instill some discipline to them. In this way, they know that their negative actions have negative consequences. It will not be easy to know when to use which measure. You will need to find your own process of teaching your kids discipline. There are many parenting books you can learn from. Or you can even learn from your mistakes. But know that you do all these things out of love for your children and your desire to help them succeed later on in life.

Give them responsibilities

At an early age, already train your children to take up some responsibility. When children feel that they have something important to do and that they can contribute to the family, they feel more impelled to learn. While they are growing up, give them household tasks such as fixing their own bed, keeping their clothes clean, storing their toys properly, sweeping the floor or washing dishes. You are not punishing your children in this way; you are helping them succeed in life by teaching them discipline. When they are able to feel responsible at a young age, they carry that sense of initiative for the rest of their lives. The home is a good training ground for them later on in life.

Make the responsibilities appropriate to their capacity. Smaller children can deal with simpler responsibilities; older children can handle more complex ones. Children will not learn from these experiences if the responsibilities are not appropriate for their capacity. They may feel over or underwhelmed when given a responsibility not apt for their age. Later on, they may carry heavier responsibilities until such time when you can even treat them as peers.

The value of responsibility is indispensable to any process of transferring knowledge and wealth to future generations. When we feel responsible, we feel that we are involved in an enterprise. There is a sense of ownership of the task because you are responsible for it. And this is something you can teach your children, little by little parents who forget to make children responsible often regret this in their older ages. Part of the failure of children in their adult lives can be blamed for poor parenting.

Give time to listen

Contrary to the notion that you should be speaking all the time to your children, you should practice more active listening with them. Yes, children go and on, babbling about everything and anything under the sun. It can get irritating at times, especially when you are tired from work and you have many things still to do. But children too need to be listened to, no matter how tired you are or meaningless their babble is. Listening to them will make them feel that they are important enough to be heard. When you listen, children feel that they are being given attention to, that they are loved enough. More than teaching them how to save or how to invest in stocks, children are going to remember more that their parents gave them time. The financial knowledge you can teach them will never replace the supporting attitude you have inculcated in them. When you listen to your children, you are saying that they are more valuable to you than your material values.

Listen to your children with full attention. Get to know them, their strengths and wants, their weakness and dislikes. These will help you engage them and connect to them before you can even teach them. You will learn a lot about your children when you really listen. Many parents who force their children to take care of the family business never even asked if their children wanted to do it. Perhaps they are afraid that their children will refuse. But if you have listened enough to your children, then you will understand how unique human beings they are and how as parents you can help them. You may not necessarily be passing on a business to your children. More importantly, you are passing values to them which will be more important when they are the ones making a living for themselves. Empower your children to make their own decisions while you support them. In this way, you are assured of success whatever your children decide to do. The financial freedom is greatly enhanced when you also desire the freedom of your children to be whoever they want to be.

Chapter 10: The More You Give, The More You Receive

The world's wealthiest man for some years surely has made philanthropy the center of his life's purpose. He had been on the top spot of wealthiest people of the year from 1995 to 2017, missing out only on four occasions. From co-founding Microsoft Corporation, he retired in 2014 to go full-time at the Bill and Melinda Gates Foundation. The foundation has since been listed as the world's wealthiest charitable institution. Through this foundation, a lot of help for women and girls achieving equitable opportunities in the poorest countries have gained support. The charity also caters to cancer and health research, water sanitation, agriculture, computer science and engineering research. Asked why he engages in philanthropy, to which Bill Gates replies, "We have to find a way to make the aspects of capitalism that serve wealthier people serve poorer people as well."

These philanthropists have seen that money is not the end point of all work. They have come to a point where money comes easy and the accumulation of it for the sake of accumulating is meaningless. We can never stress enough that money is not the end point but only a means to an end. The term we use in accumulating is cash flow. And as flow, we see that money is dynamic, never stagnant. It should not pool up in some bank account, accumulating on its own to forever. We kill the very essence of financial freedom when we refuse this flow of money. And the natural flow of money is from filling us in the inside until it overflows to those around us, and even those far and beyond us. The essence then of financial freedom is flow.

Philanthropists then have understood this flow and are demonstrating how to make good use of this flow. Are they simply altruists who have a genuine love for mankind when they donate money to curing cancer or to several charities that help the poor, the sick and the needy? Are philanthropist's saints that only love mankind purely without need of compensation?

Perhaps, yes. We can never discount the fact that this philanthropists are altruists, wanting just to help the world live in a better way. Being in a position of power and money has changed them that they are able to see beyond personal needs. They have the resources and they use that to transform the lives of many people who don't have the same capacity. There is great value then in giving money away because that is in itself rewarding. The act of generosity fills us with much meaning knowing that we have helped others in need.

But on the other hand, there is also some non-altruistic aspect to philanthropy. Yes, there may be purity of intention, that they really desire the betterment of others. But we cannot also discount the fact that the good thing they do actually benefits them back financially. This is the paradox of giving. The more you give, the more you actually receive. When Microsoft donates money to funding cancer research, it is helping build the image of a relevant and compassionate company. This may entice consumers to believe in the product more, knowing that the money they purchase the products with are going to some good use. Philanthropy then translates to sales.

Other billionaires have also pledged support to various charities and foundation. Carlos Slim Helu has his own foundation, named after himself, which supports cataract surgeries in Peru, microfinances in Colombia and education programs in Mexico. Jeff Bezos' philanthropic efforts are directed towards the advancement of scientific research. He has contributed sizable donations to the Innovation Center at the Seattle Museum of History and Industry, the Fred Hutchinson Cancer Research Center, the WorldReader and the recovery of two Saturn V engines from the Atlantic Ocean. His contributions have helped advance scientific knowledge which may have a direct or indirect impact on Bezos' industries.

In a way, we may not be billionaires as they are, but we can still practice philanthropy in our own small ways. We must always revisit our goals and objectives, making money not as an end, but as a tool for an end we want to achieve. That end may be to solve a particular problem in our community, to aid particular less-fortunate people or simply to add in our understanding of the world or simply to volunteer in some charity work. We must let money flow because we believe in principle that it will always flow back to us. This dynamism of wealth then will empower not just us, but all the people we will be able to help, creating a ripple effect of financial freedom.

Conclusion

All of the stories we have featured here talk about billionaires and their secrets to success. Some of them have started out with meager means while some were born into moneyed families. The businesses they engaged in covered most of the world's leading companies, dominating almost all important aspects of our lives. On the one hand, we may be intimidated with their wealth and status, thinking to ourselves that we may never be like them. If you are of this mind-set, then you will never really be like them. On the other hand, we may choose to learn from their lives, imitate their approach to financial freedom, and resonate with their passion to help others. They are not really different from all of us. They too are limited in their own ways. They have encountered challenges that they needed to hurdle. And right now, they are still struggling to pursue their life mission. Limited as they are, they have used the power of imagination, persistence and consistency to guide their actions. They have done the impossible because they have not thought of it as impossible.

You may be just new in the working force, eager to find your place in the sun. You may be currently frustrated with your work but just enduring the everyday to pay the bills. You may have reached your retirement but you still feel lost about the future. Do not worry. What this book perhaps offers you is a hope that things need not be the way it is. This book offers you hope, an optimistic future where you can be financially free. All it takes is a recognition that you want to change, that you are not satisfied with the limitations you have set for yourself.

Changing will not be easy. Once you follow this book, you will experience a lot of challenges, both from yourself and from those around you. At times you may even feel alone in your struggle. But use this book as your companion in your journey towards financial freedom. Believe in yourself as we believe in you. Only with hope and courage can you transform your life into one that is more wealth, more successful, and more meaningful.

Leave a Review

As an independent author with a small marketing budget, reviews are my livelihood. If you enjoyed this book, I'd really appreciate your honest feedback. You can do so by leaving a review on this book's page on Amazon. I love hearing from my readers and I personally read every single review.

https://becomingwealthyandhappy.com/fpp2ff-amz-review-ebook